CREATIVE
STITCHERY
An Introductory Guide

This book is dedicated to
Alec and Betty
for their support, enthusiasm and
encouragement

Jeannie Walker

CREATIVE
STITCHERY

An Introductory Guide

Principal photographer James Garaghty
Illustrations by Jacques le Roux

NH
NEW
HOLLAND

ACKNOWLEDGEMENTS

My sincere thanks to the following friends for shared
enthusiasm, and assistance: Norma, Faith, Jack, Lily, Janetta,
Margie, Sophie, Christine, Avery and many others.

All the photographs in this book were taken by James Garaghty,
except for the following:
Susan Abraham: p 50 (right); p 51. Jules Pasacovitch: p 28 (right,
top and bottom); p 29; p 48; p 50 (top). Michael Wyeth: p 19
(left); p 28 (left).

First published in the United Kingdom 1989 by
New Holland (Publishers) Ltd
37 Connaught Street
London W2 2AZ

Text © 1989 Jeannie Walker
Copyright © 1989 New Holland (Publishers) Ltd

Editor Annlerie van Rooyen
Designer Janice Evans

Typesetting by Diatype Setting cc
Reproduction by Unifoto Ltd
Printing and binding by National Book Printers

ISBN 1 85368 070 2

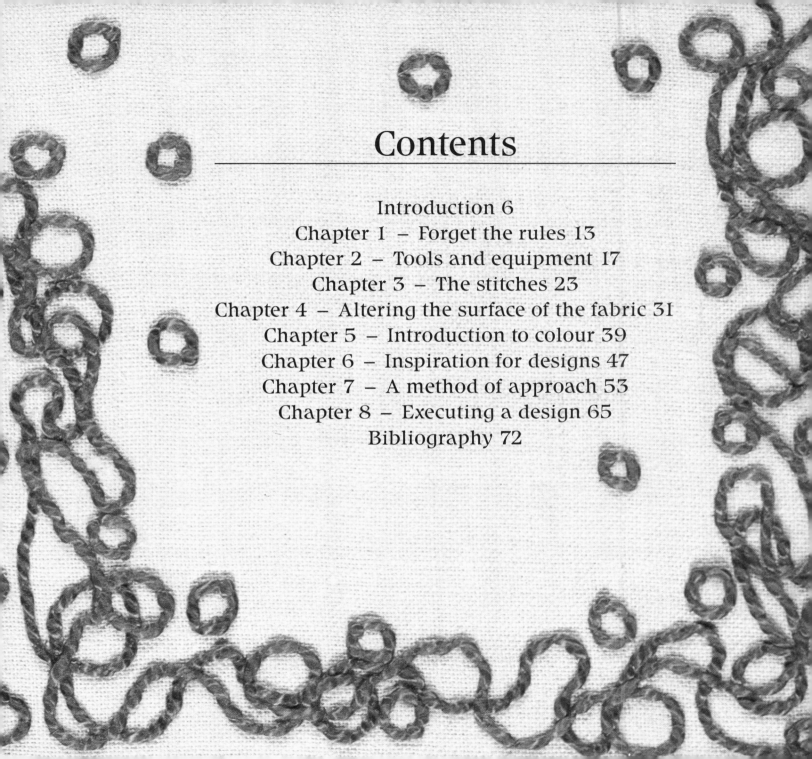

Contents

Introduction 6
Chapter 1 – Forget the rules 13
Chapter 2 – Tools and equipment 17
Chapter 3 – The stitches 23
Chapter 4 – Altering the surface of the fabric 31
Chapter 5 – Introduction to colour 39
Chapter 6 – Inspiration for designs 47
Chapter 7 – A method of approach 53
Chapter 8 – Executing a design 65
Bibliography 72

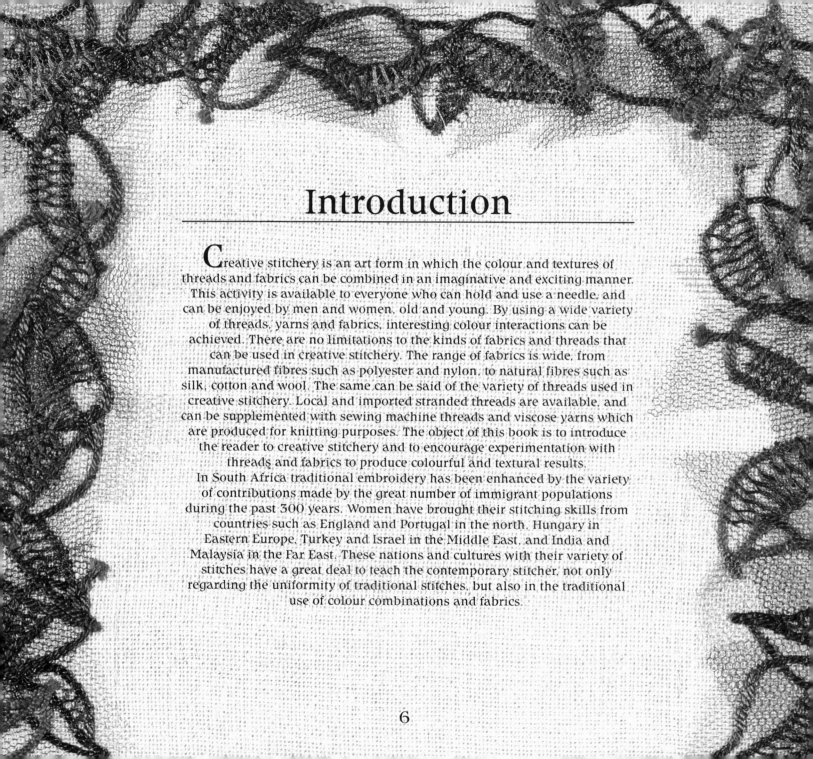

Introduction

Creative stitchery is an art form in which the colour and textures of threads and fabrics can be combined in an imaginative and exciting manner. This activity is available to everyone who can hold and use a needle, and can be enjoyed by men and women, old and young. By using a wide variety of threads, yarns and fabrics, interesting colour interactions can be achieved. There are no limitations to the kinds of fabrics and threads that can be used in creative stitchery. The range of fabrics is wide, from manufactured fibres such as polyester and nylon, to natural fibres such as silk, cotton and wool. The same can be said of the variety of threads used in creative stitchery. Local and imported stranded threads are available, and can be supplemented with sewing machine threads and viscose yarns which are produced for knitting purposes. The object of this book is to introduce the reader to creative stitchery and to encourage experimentation with threads and fabrics to produce colourful and textural results.

In South Africa traditional embroidery has been enhanced by the variety of contributions made by the great number of immigrant populations during the past 300 years. Women have brought their stitching skills from countries such as England and Portugal in the north, Hungary in Eastern Europe, Turkey and Israel in the Middle East, and India and Malaysia in the Far East. These nations and cultures with their variety of stitches have a great deal to teach the contemporary stitcher, not only regarding the uniformity of traditional stitches, but also in the traditional use of colour combinations and fabrics.

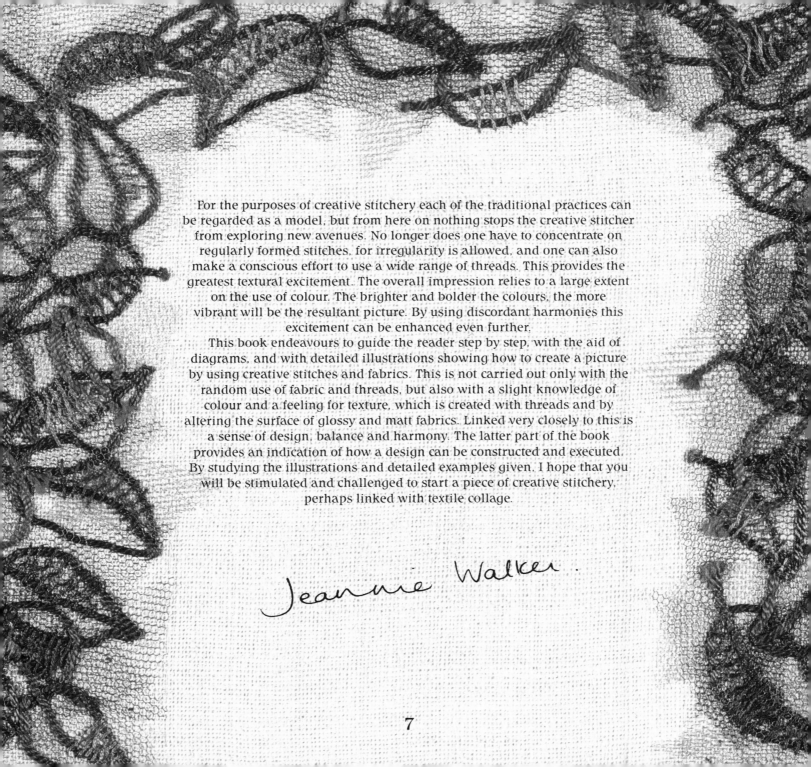

For the purposes of creative stitchery each of the traditional practices can be regarded as a model, but from here on nothing stops the creative stitcher from exploring new avenues. No longer does one have to concentrate on regularly formed stitches, for irregularity is allowed, and one can also make a conscious effort to use a wide range of threads. This provides the greatest textural excitement. The overall impression relies to a large extent on the use of colour. The brighter and bolder the colours, the more vibrant will be the resultant picture. By using discordant harmonies this excitement can be enhanced even further.

This book endeavours to guide the reader step by step, with the aid of diagrams, and with detailed illustrations showing how to create a picture by using creative stitches and fabrics. This is not carried out only with the random use of fabric and threads, but also with a slight knowledge of colour and a feeling for texture, which is created with threads and by altering the surface of glossy and matt fabrics. Linked very closely to this is a sense of design, balance and harmony. The latter part of the book provides an indication of how a design can be constructed and executed. By studying the illustrations and detailed examples given, I hope that you will be stimulated and challenged to start a piece of creative stitchery, perhaps linked with textile collage.

Jeannie Walker.

From left to right: Bedouin embroidery with fine cross stitches; Cretan stitch on a piece of embroidery which originates from Eastern Europe and is nearly a 100 years old; Roumanian couching from Eastern Europe.

Opposite page: Sampler from England on which girls practised every possible stitch they would later need to embroider clothes. This piece was completed by a certain Mary Ferry in 1796.
Left: Traditional Israeli tallith, nearly 50 years old and embroidered with straight stitch.
Below: Indian embroidery with an interesting collection of Tibetan animal figures on the foreground made from old pieces of Indian fabric.

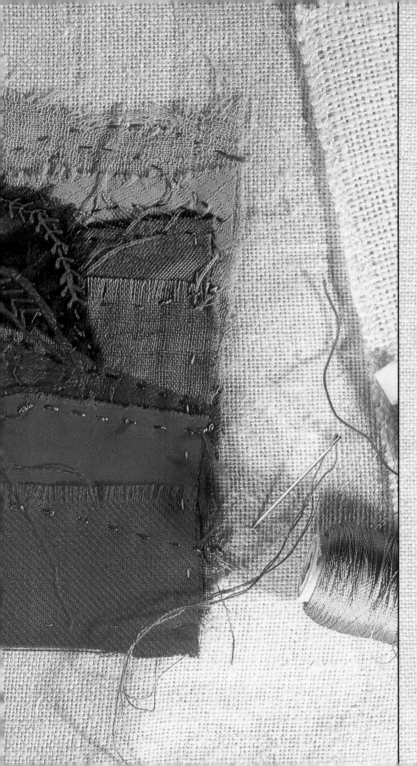

CHAPTER 1

Forget the rules

The success of creative stitchery depends very largely on how important a role creativity plays in it. This implies a questioning or even disregarding of the various rules held dear by the purists and the traditional embroiderers. Although you can still use traditional practices as a basis for your projects, the fascination of creative stitchery lies in exploring new possibilities and finding innovative solutions to problems – there are in fact no limits to the ways and means in which you can translate colours, fabric and textures into unique pieces of art. The golden 'rule' to remember is – forget the rules – there is always something new to discover!

In creative stitchery, new procedures concerning tools, materials, techniques and colours are considered. To make a stitch of any kind, a sharp needle is regarded as preferable – but is it? A very loosely woven fabric can for example be 'stitched' together and embellished by using a crochet hook. In the past, girls were often criticised if they started their stitchery with a knot instead of a back stitch. In creative stitchery a knot is certainly acceptable and furthermore it is not necessary to have it at the back of the fabric! It could be on the front, and several knots placed in a cluster could even be a feature in their own right.

For the creative stitcher, knowledge of a variety of stitches is an asset, as chapter 3 shows, but any fabric can be embellished with straight stitches at different angles and in different lengths, and by using a variety of threads in a range of colours. By employing this simple technique everyone can be creative with a needle.

In the past it has been stressed that the 'best' fabric should be used for stitchery. While this is true, I would like to encourage you to use the fabric most suitable for your

With a knowledge of straight stitches and imagination anyone can be creative with a needle, from simple projects (below) to more intricate ones, perhaps also using more stitches (right).

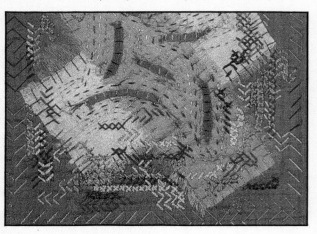

creation; there should be no restrictions. If the colour is right, but the weave of the fabric too fine for a needle with a thick thread, make holes in the fabric with an awl before poking the thick needle and thread through the fabric. However, if this is done on an extensive scale, with the accent on creating a highly textured surface, care must be taken as too much pulling could result in a slightly gathered fabric. When this happens, no amount of stretching will help the fabric to lie flat. You could of course think of cutting the threads causing the problem; the loose threads would create a further decorative dimension which perhaps you had not anticipated. An alternative is to use a frame or hoop from the outset.

Purists and traditional quilters and patchworkers generally hide the edges of the small pieces of fabric with a thin band of zigzag stitchery on the sewing machine, with a decorative stitch, or with a neat hem stitch with the edges tucked in. Other approaches are to cut the fabric deliberately to reveal either stitches or fabric below, or to fray the edges to give a 'soft focus' line to the piece of appliqué. Also, instead of randomly following the cut edge with overstitching, stitch on and off the cut edge using decorative hand and/or machine stitching (see page 12-13).

Various writers have put forward many 'rules' in stitchery and on the use of colourful fabric and threads. Each must be re-examined, for a great amount of experimentation could make your work visually much more exciting. You could consider using fabric or threads with clashing colours. For example, try some stitching with threads of red and green twisted together in one needle. One by one, try blue and orange, blue and yellow, blue and red, blue and green, and blue and mauve. The number of combinations is almost endless. The aim is to find the greatest vibration of threads reacting on the fabric that has been chosen.

Many books have been published on the craft or art form of stitchery and fabric collage. On reading them, you could query each of the rigid suggestions, and endeavour to find an alternative solution to the problems posed by the authors.

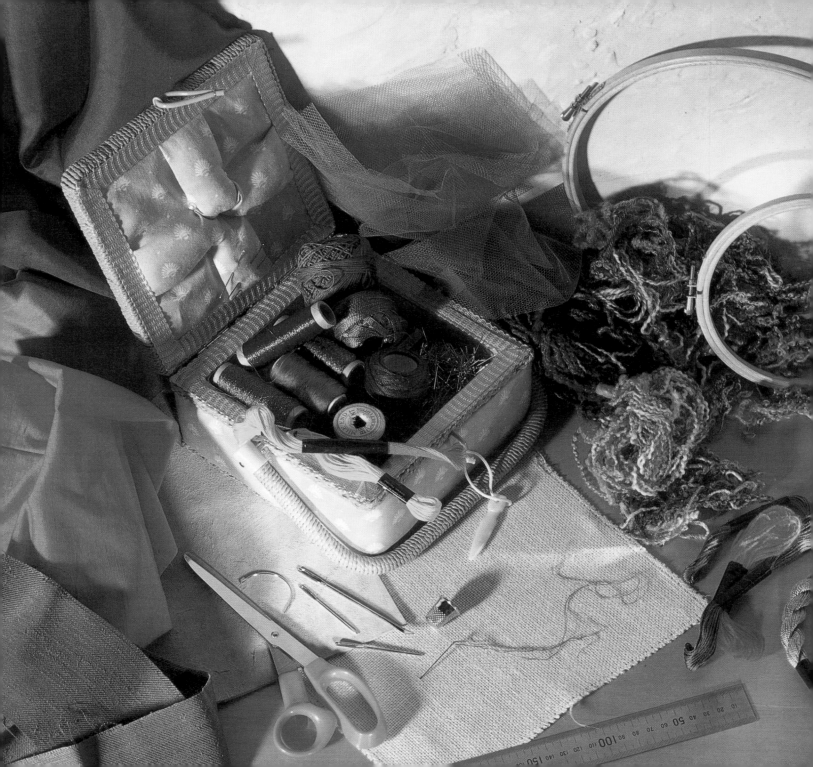

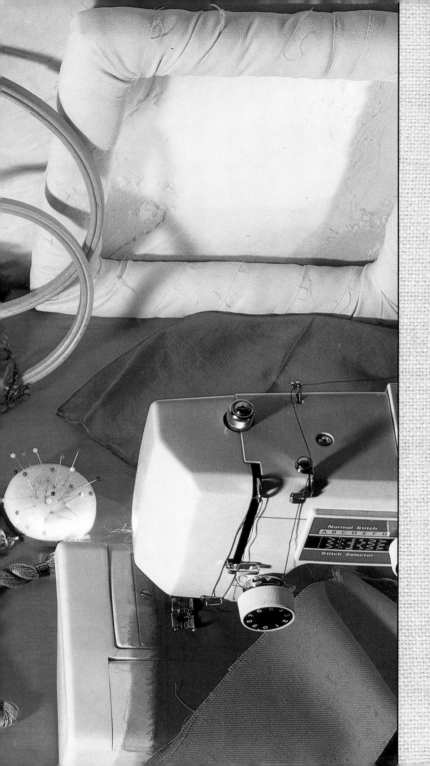

CHAPTER 2

Tools and equipment

Most homes will generally have the basic equipment at hand for creative stitchery. This includes a variety of tools such as needles, pins, a thimble (if you wish to use one), and scissors. Threads are most essential, but the beginner could use string or knitting yarns, while loosely woven fabrics are ideal for practising stitches. Basic designing equipment is generally available too, in the form of pencils, a ruler, crayons, fibre-tip pens or water-colour paints, paint brushes and paper. Only when you become more experienced and ambitious will you need to increase the quantity and perhaps the quality of threads and fabrics to incorporate into your designs.

Creative stitchery equipment

To practise stitches initially, the best needle to use is a tapestry, chenille or crewel needle with thick threads. All three are designed with a medium to large eye, and either a blunt point for tapestry work or a sharp point, as in chenille or crewel needles. These needles can easily accommodate thick yarns or threads and penetrate loosely woven fabrics. A thinner needle with a small eye is known as a 'sharp'. This is used for finer sewing and is ideal for stitching fabrics together with fine sewing threads. For attaching beads to fabric it is best to use a beading needle, which is extra fine and long. If you are a beginner without a variety of needles at hand, perhaps it would be worthwhile to buy a 'variety' pack, which contains a range of all the needles that will be required.

Pins are necessary for pinning pieces of fabric together while working on them. Fine, thin dressmaker's pins are better than the thicker variety, especially when working with delicate and firmly woven fabrics. Thicker pins will puncture the fabric and will sometimes leave a permanent mark (which you can of course hide with stitches).

A sharp pair of scissors is a basic requirement and will be sufficient until more intricately cut edges are required. At a later stage a pair of dressmaker's shears might be more desirable, as well as a small pair of embroidery scissors which are identified by their fine, long, pointed blades and which are most suitable for cutting threads.

Some stitchers use a thimble or a home-made leather or chamois finger guard. Others find working with such devices an irritation and prefer to manage without. This is a personal choice. I do not use one, but I do end up with a sore finger now and again!

Without threads you really cannot get going! As your enthusiasm grows, so will the variety of threads which you may wish to use. To make simple experimental stitches, something as basic as string, knitting wool, or four strands of sewing thread is all you need to get the 'feel' of the various stitches. Once you have become more familiar with creative stitching, you can start looking at the wide range of cotton, linen, silk, viscose, acrylic and metallic threads available to use on wall hangings, smaller pieces meant for framing, or on clothing.

Cotton threads are the most readily available and simple to use. They come in a great many forms such as sewing thread, coton à broder, soft embroidery cotton, crochet and knitting cottons. All these have a matt appearance. Cotton perlé and stranded cottons have a more lustrous sheen. Stranded threads are made up of six fine strands and can be used singly or in multiples of your choice. A wide variety of colours in this thread type is available.

Another medium suitable for stitchery is the wide range of fine to thick yarns used for tapestry and knitting purposes. Bold and richly textured effects can be created with wools, especially the weaving wools which are sometimes multicoloured and textured. Acrylic yarns in many forms are highly suitable, including knitting ribbons, which add texture and lustre to embroidery.

There is also a wide range of specialty threads such as silk, linen and viscose stitchery threads, viscose knitting yarns and metallic threads. All of these add richness whether they are used for hand sewing or on the sewing machine.

For those of you who are bold and adventurous, do not stop at using threads found on spools or in skeins: use thin strips of fabric, plastic, chamois leather and braid, each of which will produce a highly textured surface.

For practising stitches, choose a more loosely woven fabric such as hessian (burlap), or something with a similar weave. This type of fabric allows the needle with a thick thread to slide through easily. Practise on firm paper for an alternative surface. After the initial stages of experimentation, transferring to finer fabrics will be effortless.

Once you start any piece of creative stitchery, do think of using a backing fabric, such as a well-washed, thin, unbleached calico or well-worn, old sheeting. Both of these fabrics allow the needle to slip through the layers easily, and will prevent finer fabrics from distorting under the pressure of needle and threads.

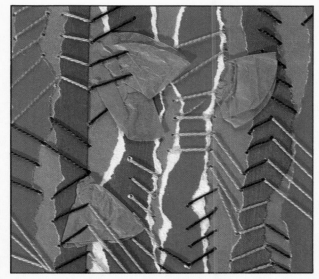

Above: Practising on paper gives you the opportunity to work on alternative surfaces.
Left: Try dying some fabrics yourself, especially chamois leather which yields very exciting results.

The range of fabrics suitable for the creative stitcher is endless. Choice of fabric will to a large extent be determined by the design, but it is only with experimentation that one can discover which suits one's needs best. Be aware of the qualities of thick and thin, matt and glossy fabrics, as well as transparent fabrics that allow the colours beneath them to alter their original colour or tone. Net, organdie, silk organza and georgette are just some of the fabrics which can be used to advantage in this way.

Should you not be able to find fabric of the colour you wish to use, what about dyeing it yourself? Natural fibres like silk absorb dyes in an exciting manner and produce rewarding results, but man-made fibres may be disappointing in this respect. The best advice is to experiment. For unusual effects, try dyeing chamois leather. With a medium to generous quantity of dyeing powder, rich colours can be obtained.

One important hint – never scorn gifts of scraps and oddments of fabric. Each piece will become valuable at some stage of your design and stitching endeavours.

The wooden frame, like the thimble, is an aid to some but a hindrance to others. It is useful when handling large pieces of work, for by firmly stretching fabric within or over a frame, the fabric will be kept reasonably taut and minimal or no puckering can occur. Rectangular or square frames can be made at home, but can also be bought, as can round or oval hoops or tambour frames.

Design equipment

The range of materials for designing is wide, but for those who are starting their experience in design, only a few basic materials are necessary. These are HB or 2B pencils, a rubber or eraser, ruler and, for colouring, pencil or wax crayons, fibre-tip pens, or water-colour or poster paints. For the latter, only the primary colours – red, blue and yellow – are necessary, with perhaps black and white for making colours darker or lighter. Sometimes the combination of blue and yellow paint does not give the required green, in which case you should buy a green of your choice. To

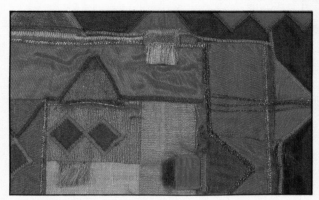

Above: A colourful piece from scraps of fabric.
Right: Design equipment which you might need.

apply paint, fine and medium paintbrushes will be sufficient. Finally, you will need drawing paper and tracing paper. The latter has a twofold use, not only for tracing designs and transferring them to fabric, but also making the templates or shapes that will be used to cut out replicas in fabric in order to make up a fabric collage.

When planning designs initially, it is best to do some preliminary work in sketch form, using the colouring medium of your choice to serve as a guideline throughout the progression of your work.

For the enthusiastic creative stitcher, a most valuable asset will be a file or scrap-book for storing drawings, sketches (even the hasty ones) and the colour exercises on paper and cloth. Collect any imagery and colour combinations that you may see in magazines. Photocopy material from books that you are unable to sketch. All of the above will provide ideas for subject matter when you need it in the future.

As can be seen from this chapter, one can start experimenting with creative stitchery by using only a few basic pieces of equipment. However, I do hope that the early exercises will greatly increase your enthusiasm, which will automatically lead to a wider range of tools, fabrics, threads and design equipment being obtained.

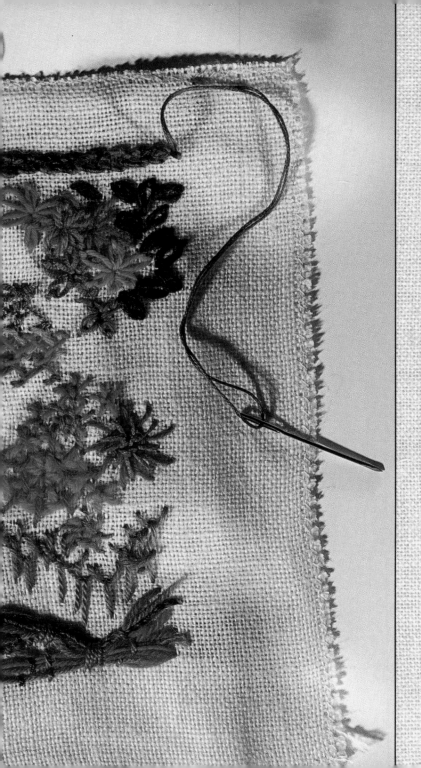

CHAPTER 3

The stitches

A needle, thread and fabric are all you need to put creative stitchery into practice. It is the variety of ways in which stitches can be applied that adds interest to a design, whether it is placed on plain cloth or on a fabric collage. Each of the basic stitches presented in this chapter is described for a specific reason. They are surface stitches, which means that the bulk of the design of the stitch is at the front of the work with minimal thread seen at the back. Experiment as much as you can right from the outset, using thin and thick, matt and glossy threads to discover the design potential of each stitch.

Some useful stitches

Stitches described hereafter are divided into three groups, the first being the straight stitches which are accomplished by putting a needle up and down through the fabric. The second group is based on those stitches which require a loop around the needle, while the third group, which has been restricted to two stitches, is very useful for creating textures.

There are, of course, many more stitches to be found in comprehensive manuals on the subject. On close study, you will notice that they are generally created from the basic stitches to be presented here. The few that are illustrated will be sufficient for most needs, and in time you will probably find that you are comfortable working with three or four stitches and generally not use the rest. Personally, I enjoy Cretan stitch most, for with it textures and tonal variations with coloured threads can be created with ease.

Each of the illustrations on page 26-27 shows the pattern of the stitches on the front and on the back of the work. The latter is mainly to assist those who are unfamiliar with the craft of stitchery.

Group One: Straight stitches

Straight stitches are the simplest of stitches and can be used very creatively. By simply taking a thread up and down through the surface of the fabric a wealth of random designs can be achieved.

Running stitch can be placed in straight lines with stitches at regular or irregular intervals, depending on the effect required. Variations on this include: *satin stitch*, with straight stitches worked regularly side by side; the traditional *long and short stitch*; and *seeding stitch*, which consists of small straight stitches placed irregularly within an area. Seeding stitch is valuable for its textural qualities as well as for slightly altering the tonal colour of one area in relation to another.

Stem stitch is used for creating lines. Textures can be created by using thin and thick threads side by side. Bring the thread out of the fabric, and working from left to right, make a stitch laterally, then bring the needle up again about mid-way between the thread and the needle insertion point. Keeping the thread always on the same side of the needle, repeat this process so that a rope-like stitch is produced. If a wider line is required, place the needle at an angle through the fabric.

Back stitch is somewhat similar to stem stitch in that it creates a line. Bring the thread up through the fabric and make a small backward stitch. Take the needle forward under the fabric to emerge one stitch length ahead of the first. Insert the needle at the point where the first stitch started and repeat the process, keeping the stitches as even as possible.

Cross stitch can be approached in two ways. If an individual stitch is required, then cross two diagonal straight stitches. If you want a line of cross stitches it is best to do it in two phases. The first is to move from one direction to another by making diagonal stitches. This forms the first half of the cross. The second phase completes the crosses by making diagonal stitches in the opposite direction.

Herringbone stitch can be used for creating textures as well as making a band for decorative purposes. Start from the left, bring the thread out of the fabric, insert the needle above to the right and make a small stitch to the left. Bring the thread downwards diagonally across and make another small stitch in the same manner. With this stitch the needle must always point to the left while working to the right. The thread must always be to the right of the needle.

Cretan stitch is remarkably similar to herringbone stitch. The difference lies in the vertical instead of the horizontal placing of the needle. To make this stitch, bring the thread through the fabric and diagonally upwards to make a small stitch with the needle pointing downwards.

The second part of this stitch is made by taking the thread diagonally down, and making a small stitch with the needle pointing upwards away from you. Make sure that the thread is at all times on the right side of the needle. Textures are created by varying the length of the diagonal and short stitches, as well as the width between each stitch.

Group Two: Stitches formed with a loop

Chain stitch can be worked as a line as well as in the form of individual stitches. Bring the thread up through the fabric. Holding the thread down with your left thumb, insert the needle where it last emerged. Bring the point out a short distance away, keeping the thread under the needle and ensuring that it encircles the needle from left to right. Finally, complete a line of chain stitches with a small stitch to prevent it unravelling.

Feather stitch is an open chain stitch made alternately to the left and to the right of an invisible centre line. Bring the thread through the fabric, hold the thread down and insert the needle a little bit to the right on the same level. Make a stitch down to the centre, ensuring that the thread is kept under the needle. Now insert the needle a little bit to the left on the same level and make a stitch to the centre, keeping the thread under the needle. Textures can be achieved by working this stitch loosely, and an interesting addition can be made by working another line on top of the first.

Buttonhole stitch is a further variation of the looped stitch, and is generally used as an edging stitch since the lower edge of the stitch forms a solid line. Bring the thread out of the fabric. With the needle pointing downwards and keeping the thread under the needle, make a straight stitch, with the needle emerging on the same line as the initial point. Finally complete a line of buttonhole stitches with a small stitch to prevent distortion of the last stitch. This stitch is generally worked from left to right.

Fly stitch can be worked individually or used as a decorative band. In making separate fly stitches, bring the thread up through the fabric. Insert the needle a little distance away from where it first emerged on the same level. Holding the thread downwards make a diagonal stitch to the centre with the needle at right angles to the thread. Catch the loop in the centre by a short or long straight stitch according to your design. When making a band of fly stitches, place them together regularly or irregularly depending on the desired effect.

Group Three: Stitches used for creating textures

French knots are made by twisting the thread around the needle and securing it. Bring the thread up through the fabric and, holding it with the left thumb, encircle the thread once or twice with the needle in an anti-clockwise direction. Reinsert the needle close to the starting point. At this point, hold the knot gently under your thumb as you pull the thread through the fabric. Loose knots are as interesting as those that have been formed traditionally, and *en masse* they can add a further dimension to textured work.

Couching can be used for outlining or filling in an area. The principle of couching is to secure a thicker or decorative element such as metal thread, cords, ribbons, as well as strips of chamois leather and fabric, with small, near-invisible stitches, or perhaps any of the stitches that I have described above. The element to be couched down can be held to the fabric by a stitch at the start and by securing the loose end, either by pulling it through the fabric at a point dictated by the design, or by holding it down with pins throughout. Make small upright stitches or other stitches of your choice, such as cross stitch or fly stitch, over the thicker element. Bound bundles of threads can be couched down to form a highly textured and colourful area.

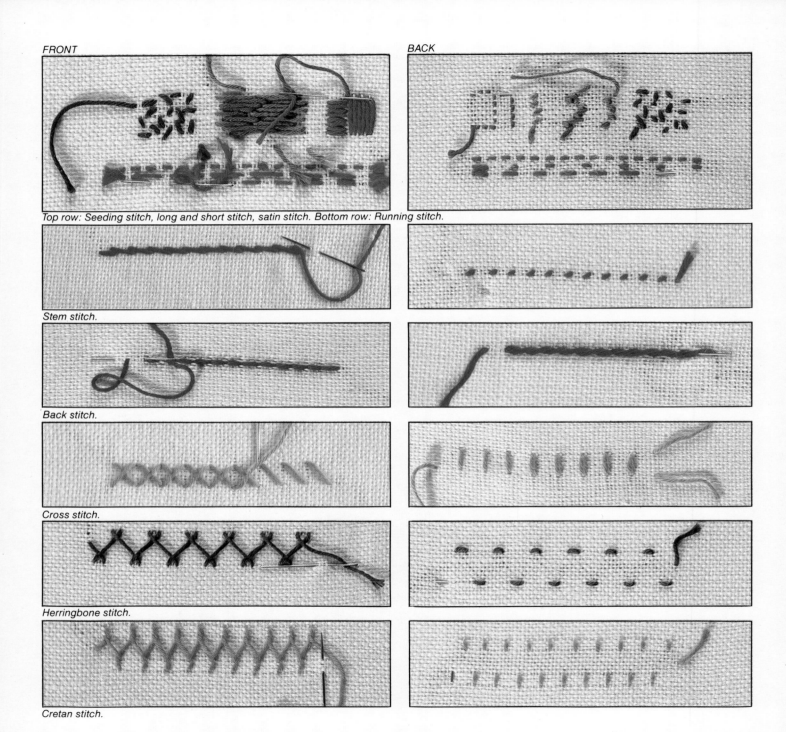

FRONT

BACK

Top row: Seeding stitch, long and short stitch, satin stitch. Bottom row: Running stitch.

Stem stitch.

Back stitch.

Cross stitch.

Herringbone stitch.

Cretan stitch.

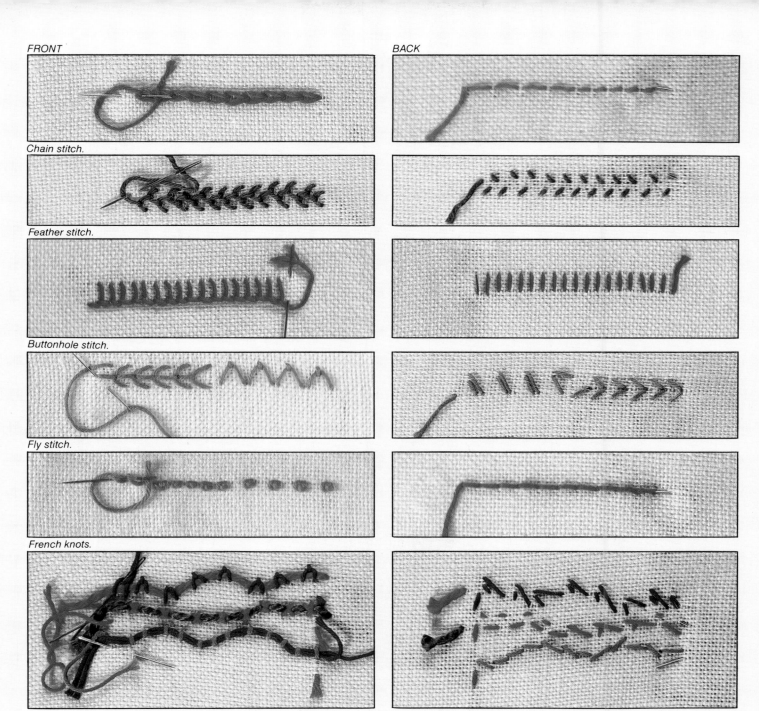

FRONT

BACK

Chain stitch.

Feather stitch.

Buttonhole stitch.

Fly stitch.

French knots.

Couching.

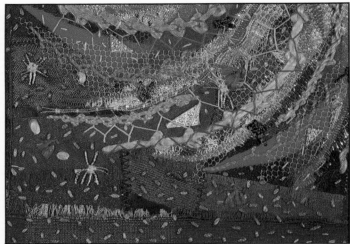

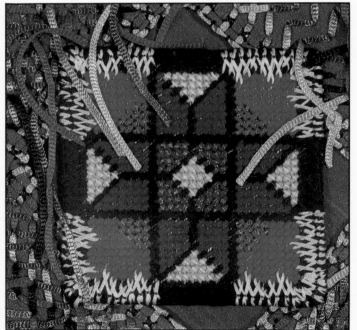

Details of stitches on chamois leather (left), Fireworks (top) and a project with a Ndebele motif (above).

The sewing machine

In the past, sewing machine embroidery was considered to be inferior to creative hand stitchery. Recently this view has been dispelled by highly creative designers and embroiderers who have demonstrated exceptional skills on the sewing machine in the field of textile art.

The sewing machine is highly recommended for embellishing fabric. Even the most limited of hand-operated sewing machines can be used to make stitch designs. More common is the electric sewing machine which can do straight and zigzag stitching, and is entirely adequate for all creative stitchery. The most important feature is that it leaves your hands free to manipulate or to guide the fabric, with or without the use of a circular frame.

Certain facilities on your sewing machine will enable you to achieve exciting results. The first is the machine's ability to 'free stitch'. This is done by removing the foot, and lowering or covering the feed dog. A speed regulator set to slow or medium is preferable for greater control. Sometimes it is wise to loosen the bobbin or spool tension; yet in some sewing machines this is not possible and a second bobbin case producing the desired tension may be required. Should you have any doubts about the potential of your sewing machine, consult the manufacturer.

For early experimental exercises, place fabric, such as calico, tautly into a circular embroidery frame; remove the foot of the sewing machine, lower the feed dog and set the zigzag and stitch regulator at zero. Place the frame beneath the threaded needle, put the presser lever down, and set the machine at a slower speed. Then pull the bobbin thread up through the fabric, hold it, and with the sewing machine in action, gently guide the frame backwards, forwards, sideways and in a circular motion so that you can see what your machine can do.

Bear in mind that it is the user who creates the effects, and that the sewing machine must only be regarded as a tool in obtaining the desired results.

This work shows that a sewing machine can be used very successfully to decorate stitchery projects.

29

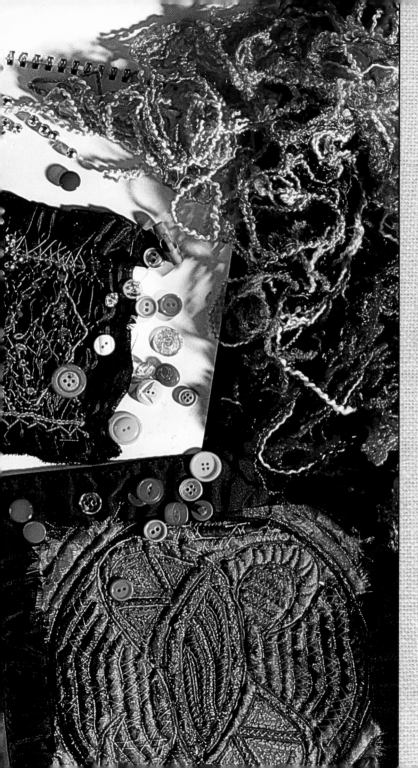

CHAPTER 4

Altering the surface of the fabric

Part of the pleasure of working with fabric in creative stitchery is its wide potential for being manipulated. Construction of warp and weft threads allows most fabrics to be frayed, stretched, pleated, folded, tucked, gathered and twisted generally without it disintegrating. In this lies its uniqueness. The extent to which it can be manipulated depends on the structure of the woven cloth. The potential of a loose weave such as in linen, hessian (burlap) and muslin (cheesecloth) will differ from that of satin, taffeta and fine cotton. Shallow three-dimensional effects can be obtained by padding the whole or part of the surface. These techniques are traditionally known as English quilting, Italian or corded quilting and trapunto. They can be used in conjunction with those mentioned above, and embellished with surface stitchery, either by hand or on the sewing machine. When combined, these techniques can create a richly textured surface.

Fraying

Fabric can be attractively frayed to create effects in a collage. To do this, simply unravel the woven warp and weft threads. All fabrics do not fray in the same manner. Loosely woven threads fray far more rapidly and easily than those of a tightly or firmly woven cloth, including knitted fabrics, which may also stretch in a manner in which some woven fabrics cannot. Frayed edges can be used to eliminate hard edges, and correspondingly yield a highly organised finish with an aura of spontaneity, which can be emphasized by ragged edges, and threads of the fabric caught down by machine stitching or by hand. To use the frayed edge to its best advantage, combine fine and loosely woven fabrics to obtain the greatest textural impact.

Always consider the function of your work. If it is to be a decorative piece to place on the wall or under glass, any amount of frayed edges will be acceptable. Should the frayed edges be part of a design to be placed on a garment, you must think about how much hand-washing or dry-cleaning the garment will be able to withstand. Harsh treatment may result in the eventual disintegration of the unprotected frayed fabric within the design.

Cut-work

There are two traditions of this technique. In the one which originates from Europe 'cut-work' describes the buttonhole stitching on the perimeter of shapes to be retained, and the cutting away of background areas. It is traditionally done in white threads on white fabric. The second technique is known as Mola work and originates from the San Blas Islands off Panama. This involves placing layers of colourful fabric one on top of the other, and then stitching and cutting according to a pre-planned design, in which each of the colours is exposed for maximum impact. In Mola work, also known as San Blas or reverse appliqué, it is customary to turn all the edges of the cut fabric under and to stitch them down neatly.

From a creative stitchery point of view, this technique is

Above: Traditional cut-work with buttonhole stitching around the edges.
Left: A striking detail of Bird Cloak *by Faith Loy Plaut, illustrating beautifully how fabric can be frayed for creative stitchery projects.*

exciting, and the need to turn under the cut edges can be eliminated by the use of the sewing machine, hand stitching, or simply by leaving the edges exposed.

Holes cut into fabric can be visually arresting when transparent fabrics are laid one over the other. Careful planning of areas to be cut away from each layer will create greater visual impact as parts of the foundation fabric will then be exposed as well as, perhaps, unplanned colourful nuances. This is best achieved with net and transparent silk fabrics such as silk organza, rather than synthetic organza, which although it appears transparent, does not always allow the coloured fabric underneath it to influence its own colour.

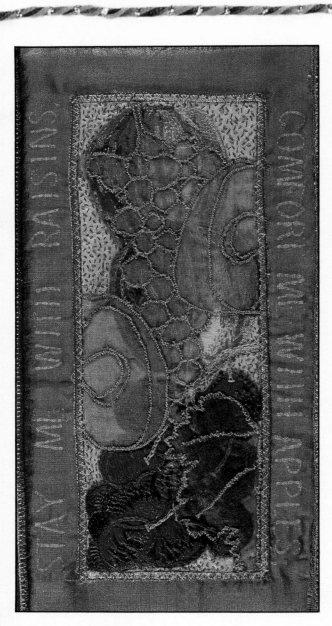

Pleats, tucks, folds and gathers

Most fabrics can be manipulated into pleats, tucks, folds and gathers. These can be decoratively used in combination with creative stitchery to enhance a collage. Each of these techniques was used by costume designers in ancient Egypt, Greece and Rome, and their decorative value is still popular today. Because of the way in which they were manufactured, synthetic fabrics have special qualities and do not respond to these techniques in the same way as natural fibres. Pleats and folds in crease-resistant fabric will produce a softly ridged appearance, while sharper edges are yielded by silk, cotton and fine linen. All of these fabrics respond well to tucking and gathering.

The visual qualities of pleating and folding can be enhanced by adding scraps of fabric in between the ridges. Unusual effects can be created by placing folds and pleats evenly and unevenly and by contrasting the direction of the ridges with wide and narrowly placed securing stitches. Multi-directional tucking can also add to the textural impact of a surface. In this case the use of the twin needle on the sewing machine is recommended for quick results, rather than working large areas by hand.

Twisted fabric

Textures can also be created by using twisted cords and ribbons of fabric. Cords can be matt or glossy and can consist of handmade braids and rouleaux (thin fabric cylinders). Frayed edges of twisted strips of fabric, including those with a two-tone effect, produce a colourful interaction within a highly textured collage. To achieve a two-tone effect, take two fabrics of contrasting tones or colours, twist them and secure with stitching at each end.

Left: A modern interpretation of cut-work.
Right: English quilting.

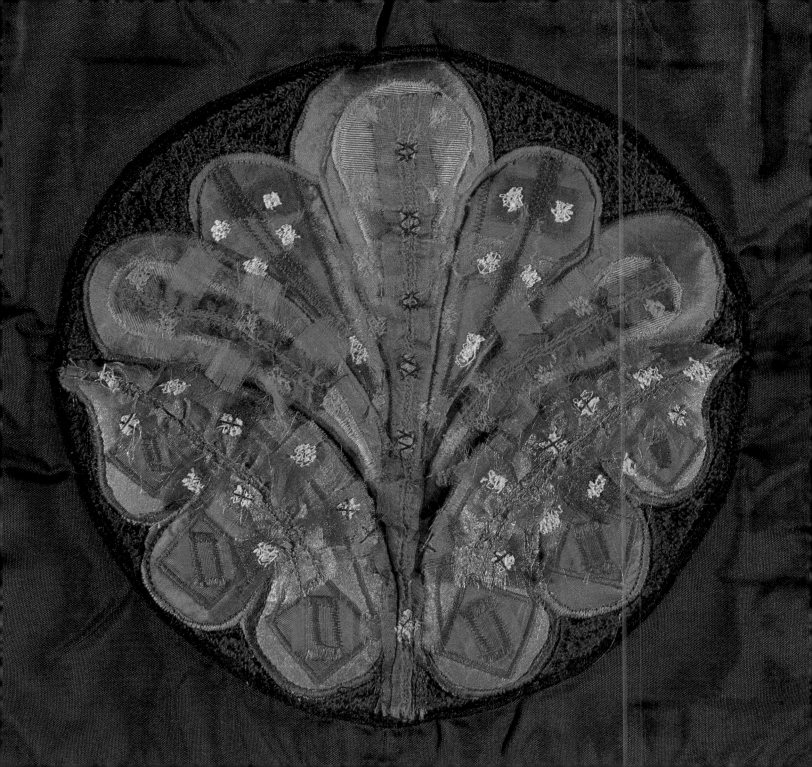

Quilting

The technique of quilting has a long history which probably started in ancient Egypt, and was used throughout the centuries by many cultures for warmth as well as to provide a thicker body covering in times of war.

Quilting entails stitching together several layers of fabric. In our own times it is associated with bedcovers, wall hangings and clothing. The technique generally associated with quilting entails two layers of fabric with a fluffed-out synthetic material known as wadding or batting in between. Stitched lines forming patterns hold the three layers together and the result is known as English quilting.

In creative stitching, quilting can be used for decorative purposes. The process is similar to traditional quilting, but you can also explore the possibilities of Italian or corded quilting and trapunto or stuffed quilting.

English quilting

This method involves quilting the entire piece of stitched work. With this in mind, it is best to assess at the planning stages whether it would be wise to work in smaller units and then to join the pieces together, as when making a garment, or to work with one large unit as when making a wall hanging. The second consideration is whether to quilt by hand or with a sewing machine. Should your design require extensive hand stitchery and textural application, then it would perhaps be best to complete this before quilting the entire work. Once it is ready for quilting, use large running stitches to tack (baste) the work through the wadding (batting) and an additional backing material, such as well-washed thin calico (muslin), to prevent wrinkling and pulling in any part of the work. A grid of tacking (basting stitches) all over the work will ensure an even distribution of the wadding. Without it, distortions can occur. At this stage, quilt the work according to your design with small running stitches, a decorative stitch or machine stitching.

Italian or corded quilting

Italian or corded quilting is a decorative quilting technique which relies on a design using narrow channels. These are created by two parallel lines of small running stitches or by machine stitching. A thick cord of either knitting wool or yarn, or even ribbons made of pantihose or tights, is threaded through these channels from the back of the work to form exaggerated ridges. This is achieved by stitching together two or more layers of fabric – one being the thin backing fabric and the other being the foundation fabric of your work. The channels must be stitched through these two layers. The width of the channels depends on your design, but could vary between four and six millimetres (¼– ⅜ inches). Once the initial quilting is finished, decorative stitching can be applied on the ridges and in the valleys created by the inserted cords.

Trapunto or stuffed quilting

In trapunto or stuffed quilting, individual areas of the design are padded, thereby emphasizing certain areas more than others. This technique is achieved by encircling the area to be padded with small running stitches through two layers of fabric, one being the backing fabric, and the other being the top foundation fabric. Turn the work over and within the delineated area make a small slit in the backing fabric only. Then stuff enough wadding (batting) into the area to highlight your design and restitch the cut with oversewing or herringbone stitch.

Surface texture of creative stitchery can be enhanced with the use of beads, buttons, feathers, grasses and rich braiding, or anything else that may take your fancy. I have seen shells and even fishbones stitched to wall hangings. For the stitching of fine beads to a fabric, you will need an extra fine needle, known as a beading needle. For the very adventurous stitcher there are no boundaries. The only limitations are self-imposed.

Right: Italian or corded quilting.

CHAPTER 5

Introduction to colour

Colour, coupled with design, is the most important element in creative stitchery. The stitched work will either vibrate with interest, or be lacking in colourful interaction. For the creative stitcher the potential of colour use is enormous. It is generally fear of the unknown that keeps people from experimenting with colour. As a result, we surround ourselves with neutral colours with perhaps a hint of bright colours when we feel a little daring. Possibly after working with colours in the form of fabrics and threads on a small scale, your appreciation of colour awareness will grow, and in time you will surprise yourself with your abilities!

The study of colour can be a highly complex scientific subject, but from the point of view of this book it is best to approach colour visually. Colour surrounds us at all times, yet rarely do we stop to analyse it. Colours have become coded: yellow butter, green grass, red blood. Our physical and emotional states are colour-coded too, for we associate blue with cold, pink with vitality, green with jealousy, red with anger, and purple with rage.

What is behind colour analysis? Studies of colour science were greatly advanced by Isaac Newton (1642-1727). He was the first to produce a separation of the rainbow colours by shining 'white' light or sunlight through a glass prism. The resulting refracted beam of light produced the spectrum (the colours of the rainbow). Newton named seven colours for his rainbow: red, orange, yellow, green, blue, indigo and violet. Actually one hardly sees indigo as a separate colour; orange too is a bit doubtful. Some think that Newton liked the number seven and added orange and indigo purely to make up the magic number!

Colour can only be observed when there is light. Look around a dark room at night to experience this. Yet when we stop to observe, we see many variations in colour, ranging from dark to light. This depends on the composition of the colours, and also, sometimes, on the position of colours in relation to a light source.

The creative stitcher might like to know that science has made a noteworthy contribution to our understanding of colour. Continual research is carried out on pigments which influence the colours of paints, inks and dyes. A great number of colours are derived from vegetable matter and coloured earths; some are natural, while others have been altered by chemical reactions. Through research colour scientists have added to the range of colours which are available at present.

Next time you see a clear rainbow, note that there are three main colours – red, blue and yellow. These are known as primary colours. In the field of pigment development a primary colour is one that is not derived from others, either by mixing or by manufacture. These three colours form the foundation of the colour wheel.

Secondary colours – green, orange and purple – are derived by mixing equal quantities of blue and yellow to produce green, red and yellow for orange, and red and blue for purple.

Tertiary colours are derived from mixing different quantities of a primary colour with a secondary colour. Thus yellow mixed with a little orange will produce yellow-orange, while more yellow than orange will lighten the tone of the orange. Orange mixed with varying quantities of red will produce varying tones of deep orange or orange-red. A similar process is followed to obtain tones of tertiary colours around the colour wheel.

Colour has a descriptive language of its own. The more the creative stitcher becomes involved with colour studies, the more apparent the terms will be. Two terms to become familiar with are hue and tone. Hue refers to a specific colour. The example shown on the right contains three shades – or hues – of green, among the great number of greens that can be mixed from blue and yellow, two of the primary colours. The tone of a colour refers to a range from near black of a colour to the lightest colour nearest to white. The darkest tones are derived from adding black, while the lightest are derived from adding white, both in varying quantities. The overall variety is known as a tonal range or tonal variation.

Colours in pairs or in groups can either vibrate against each other or harmonise. Those that vibrate against each other are known as complementary colours. Take another look at the colour wheel. Colours that complement red are green, blue and purple; those that are complementary to yellow are red, purple and blue; while those that are complementary to blue are red, orange and yellow. It will be noted that the group of colours lie directly opposite to the primary colour in question. When placing equal quantities of complementary colours side by side, the effect is raw and crude; on the other hand, if you place a small quantity of one of the primary colours upon its complementary, a vibration of colour is achieved. This element of balance can produce very rich results in creative stitchery. Analogous or similar colours are those that co-

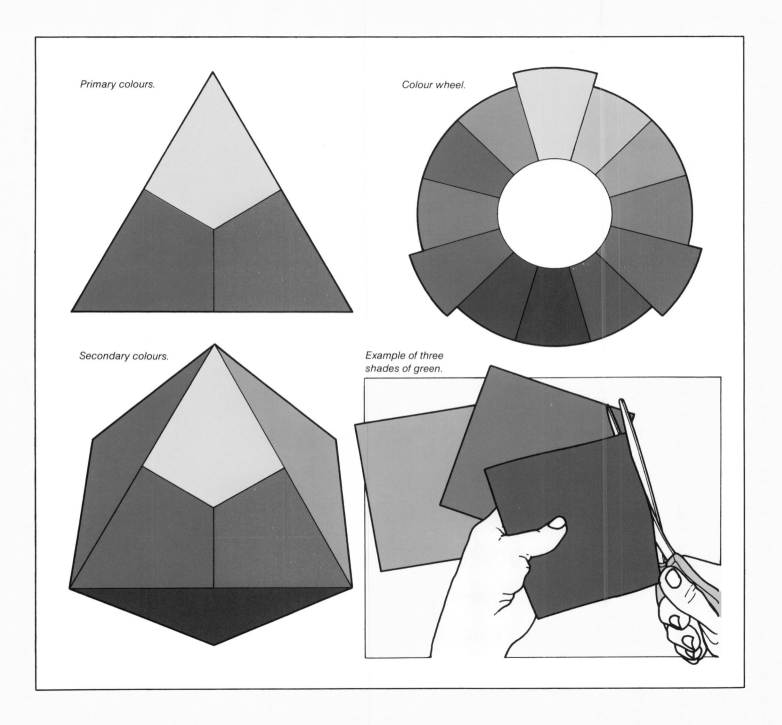

Primary colours.

Colour wheel.

Secondary colours.

Example of three
shades of green.

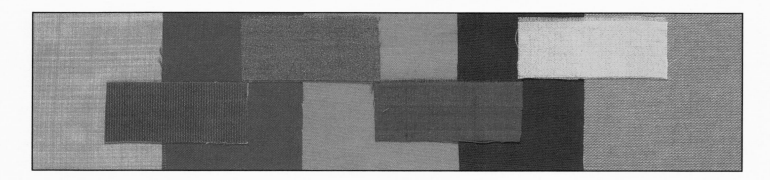

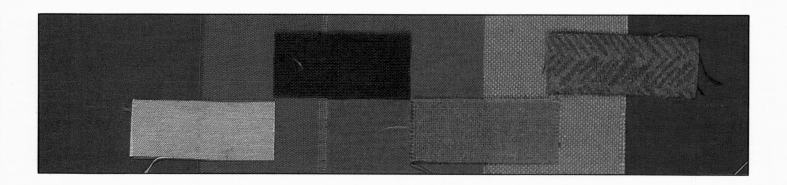

Three examples of analogous colours forming harmonious combinations.

exist harmoniously. Colours which harmonise with each other are: the blue, green, yellow range; the green, yellow, orange range; the yellow, orange, red range; and the red, purple, blue range.

Visual colour shocks are produced when small areas of 'quiet' colour are placed on a large area of saturated (vivid) colour, or vice versa. This kind of interaction takes place when a colour of near white tone is placed upon medium to dark tones. For example, when cream-coloured dots are placed upon a purple background, the viewer will immediately be aware of the dots rather than of the background colour. A better balance would be achieved by replacing the cream with a medium tone of yellow ochre. When working with fabrics and threads this sharp interaction can be corrected by working over the offending colour with appropriately coloured threads.

Colours are divided into warm and cold ranges. Warm colours are those that lie in the orange sector of the colour wheel. These include yellows, yellow-oranges, oranges, reds and purples. Cold or cool colours lie on the opposite side of the colour wheel and include yellow-greens, greens, blue-greens, blues and blue-purples.

Colours can have a great effect on us. We can be cheered, depressed, stimulated, provoked or antagonised by the volume and tones of colour within our environment. Used inappropriately, colour can cause strain and tension. When considered carefully, the use of colour can, however, enrich the environment and thereby have a positive effect on our well-being. Colour is used by everyone, yet few people think about how colours should best be used.

Insufficient interest in colour reduces our colour awareness to a hit-or-miss affair where colour choice is left to chance. However, with thought and experimentation, this tendency can be altered. People think that colour combinations can be made without placing the colours in the environment they are destined for. When making colour purchases, take your samples of fabric and threads with you in order to make an accurate assessment. It can be dangerous to try to remember colour. Artificial light can also play tricks on our eyes and our perception of colours.

A useful tip is to choose colours in daylight should you wish to use them under artificial light conditions.

To appreciate colour more intimately, try a few simple experiments or exercises on your own. Try mixing colours by using a water-colour paint-box. Actually, a child's paint-box will be adequate. For this exercise water-colour paints are better than fibre-tip pens, coloured pencils or wax-crayons. With the help of the illustrations in this chapter, try to make your own colour wheel. The most important advice is to work with untainted primary colours (red, blue and yellow); so clean them well before you start. Be careful not to contaminate the colours while you are working; keep a jar full of water and a few tissues at hand, in order to clean your paint-brush each time you use a different pigment. Paint three circles of red, blue and yellow on a piece of white paper, and around the perimeter of each add small quantities of the other two primary colours to obtain the secondary colours. The tertiary colours will be achieved by adding small quantities of primary colours to the secondary colours. To achieve a tonal variation on a specific colour, add varying quantities of black and white in stages to a colour of your choice.

If you do not own a water-colour paint-box, try using fibre-tip pens, coloured pencils or wax-crayons, although the colour mixture will not be the same. Otherwise you could try another experiment. Page through some old magazines – ones that you do not mind destroying – and tear out all the coloured illustrations, mainly advertisements, that catch your eye. When you have assembled them, cut out squares from the uniformly coloured areas, each perhaps 4 x 4 cm (1½ x 1½ in). After grouping them into colours such as blues, yellows, greens, oranges, reds and purples, arrange them into an area in order to achieve a harmonious arrangement of colour. Your eye will soon begin to tell you that if tones of a colour differ greatly they do not lie harmoniously together. Some time will be spent arranging the squares to achieve a harmonious grading. This exercise will also give you an idea of the meaning of tonal range (dark or light) and of colour saturation (a colour's degree of intensity or purity). The illustration on the

Cool colours.

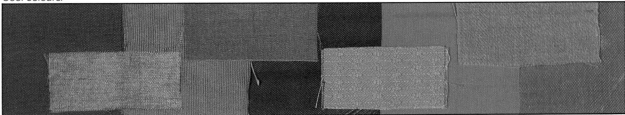

Warm colours.

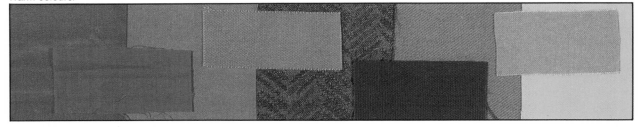

Sharp contrast with better balance of colours on the right.

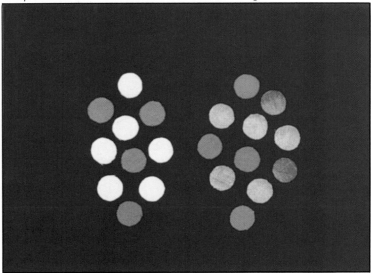

Mixing three primary colours to obtain secondary colours.

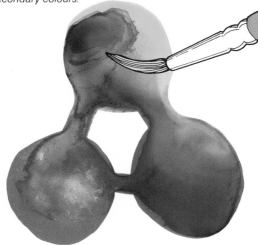

Tonal variations from dark to light.

right shows a black border around part of a block of squares. You will note that the colours along the edge appear more intense than those on the opposite edge, which are against the white paper. A dark or black surface absorbs light and so assists colours to reveal their true intensity, whereas a white surface reflects light and diminishes the intensity of the colours closest to it.

A further exercise could be to take a piece of colourful wrapping paper, fabric, or an advertisement that appeals to you, to discover the number of colours as well as the tones of colours used. To do this, you could use strips of coloured paper that correspond to the colours and tones in the piece. Should you not be able to find enough colours within the advertisements of a magazine, you could paint them, or could use fabric or threads. The object of this exercise is to assist you in identifying colours and, secondly, to show that it is the quantity of each colour that varies within the design. This ultimately illustrates that a group of exciting colours does not always produce an exciting result. It is the proportion of one colour against another and within a group that is important.

The study of colour relationships is a continuous and never-ending process. When it is possible, study some books on fine art, especially art over the past 100 years, commencing with the French Impressionists and subsequent European art movements. Take a close look at the colour application of artists like Claude Monet and Auguste Renoir, the Post-Impressionists such as Paul Gauguin and Vincent van Gogh, and the Fauve painters such as Henri Matisse, among many others. Good colour plates will reveal the balance of colour in relation to the design. Visit the local art galleries if you can, for they will give an indication of the current trends in colour thinking. Interesting colour combinations can be found in fashion magazines, as well as in magazines on interior decoration. If it is possible, cut out the ones that interest you and stick them into a scrap-book. In fact, keeping fragments of all such ideas, as well as your own experiments, is invaluable. They will all be very useful later as you progress in creating your own designs.

Colour panels will give you a better understanding of shades and tonal ranges.

Flowers and Foliage for Pressing

PRIMULA
annual: winter/spring
Press both purple and white, face-down and
in profile... becomes pale cream. Press
some buds... attached to
the caly...

PRUN...
(Brow...
tree...
Press...
a...

VINCA MAJOR (Periwinkle)
shrub or groundcover: summer
Press flat or in profile – an excellent blue.

VIOLA (Pansies and violets)
annual: winter
Small flowers can be pressed whole;
...parate the petals of larger flowers.
...as much of the stalk as possible and
...ers face down.

Pressed Flowers

RANUNCULUS
ASIATICUS

VIOLA (Violet)

ZINNIA

VINCA MAJOR

PLUMBAGO
AURICULATA

CHAPTER 6

Inspiration for designs

In the previous chapters, threads, needles, stitches, fabric and colour have been discussed. The final issue is – what to do with each of these components, and how to put creative stitchery into practice. Those with some sense of design may be inspired by the mere sight of a group of coloured threads placed against one or several colourful fabrics. The colour relationships may express a mood, or an emotion, which can be emphasized by the stitching applied to large and small areas. Even with threads and fabrics at hand, some might, however, still feel somewhat hesitant to get involved.

The suggestions I make here for creative stitching projects are by no means exhaustive, and I am sure that you will soon discover that there is no end to the areas in which you can find inspiration.

Highly motivated beginners need never feel shy or inhibited about copying a picture or finding a small area within a picture on which to base their creative stitchery projects. If you find an image that is colourfully appealing within a magazine page, a children's book illustration, a birthday or Christmas card, wrapping paper, a botanical or biological study, you could enlarge it expressly to practise colour and design relationships, and use threads and stitches in combinations. This could be a rewarding exercise for the creative stitcher. Accuracy of forms or shapes and colour is not the issue; what is important is having a visual image which has the effect of stimulating you to become involved.

The time will come when you will no longer need to look at illustrations for copying purposes, because you will feel like exploring on your own. The range of subject matter appropriate for creative stitchery becomes almost inexhaustible when considering the great number of interests, hobbies, perhaps sports such as sailing, ballooning and others, which help us to look at familiar life from a different viewpoint. For instance, the theme of water sports has led to analysing sails, ancient and modern, life on the water, weather conditions, cloud patterns, water vegetation, or plant life found at the water or ocean's edge. Marine life such as fish, shells, seaweed and coral have become popular images for creative stitchery. Insects, birds and plant-life as abstracted forms are a familiar sight and are there to be used by everyone with creative abilities.

Life and objects around the home are also aspects to be studied, from decorations and ornaments, to objects such as sweets, colourful cotton reels within a glass jar, fruit in fruit-dishes or bowls, and flowers placed in bottles of water. Perhaps you could cut open fruit and vegetables, or pull apart flowers and leaves, to have a closer look at hollows and protruding shapes, as well as the variety of colours surrounding each object. Observing shadows on flat and curved surfaces and textured objects, as well as the reflections of leaves and light on water, could also provide you with a wealth of shapes and distortions to choose from.

This work, Ndebele I, *was inspired by African designs.*

Creative stitchery themes do not have to be derived from nature study only. The world of entertainment and amusement also holds colourful possibilities. Think of the circus, magician shows, apparatus in amusement parks such as the merry-go-round, colourful tents and the flickering colours of neon lights as well as colourful computer imagery which also holds many possibilities.

Local cultures have many crafted artifacts which display a range of configurations which could be used as a point of departure for a stitchery project. Think of looking at colourful beadwork, the intricate patterns on basketry, as well as pottery and handmade masks used for ceremonial purposes. The linear forms found in the designs seen on the walls of domestic architecture is an element that should not be overlooked. It is not necessary to look only at our own cultural objects. Think too of those from ancient cultures, such as the jewellery of ancient Egypt, or the imagery on the ancient Greek vases which were black on red or vice versa. Geometric forms were colourfully interpreted in woven cloth by ancient cultures of Central America. Each craft has a rich history, with colour and forms suitable for adaptation for stitchery projects.

Playing with words, such as fireworks or goldfish, and analysing quotations from famous literature or poems where objects and situations conjure up their own imagery, have become the sources of inspiration that I appreciate most. Most people have favourite poets or authors whose words linger in the memory and subsequently have a greater meaning for them. The following are some examples that hold possibilities for creative stitchery projects.

This poem comes from the south of Spain and was possibly written in the thirteenth century.

. . . the sun reddening in the evening,
As if she clothed herself with a scarlet robe.
She strips the north and south of colour
And covers the west with purple.
And the earth she leaves naked,
Hidden in the shadow of night . . .

The works of Shakespeare, for example this extract from *The Tempest*, provide many exciting images for colour and design.

Full fathom five thy father lies:
Of his bones are coral made;
Those are pearls that were his eyes:
Nothing of him that doth fade,
But doth suffer a sea change
Into something rich and strange . . .

Short quotations from 'The Song of Solomon' from the Old Testament have been a profitable theme to me. The lines that I have chosen come from the second and fourth chapters, and each holds images that could be interpreted in many ways.

. . . For lo, the winter is past, the rain is
over and gone. The flowers appear on the earth . . .
(Chapter 2 verses 11 and 12)

. . . The time of the singing of birds is come,
and the voice of the turtle is heard in
our land . . .
(Chapter 2 verse 12)

. . . Awake, O north wind; and come thou
south; blow upon my garden, that the spices
thereof may flow out . . .
(Chapter 4 verse 16)

Books on art and crafts will always be sources of inspiration for, by looking through them in conjunction with the subject matter that you have in mind, your span of imagery will increase, as well as your understanding of colour and design. You should collect postcards, greeting cards, newspaper and magazine cut-outs and similar memorabilia, along with scraps of fabrics and threads and store them in a file or a scrap-book. The more you collect, the wider your interests and horizons will be.

Sources of inspiration for creative stitchery projects are almost inexhaustible and include anything from leaves and pods *(left)*, and playing with words like Fireworks *(below left)*, to quotations from 'The Song of Solomon' which inspired Buttercups *(below)* and Eastern Garden *(right)*.

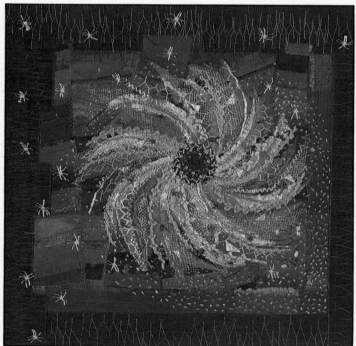

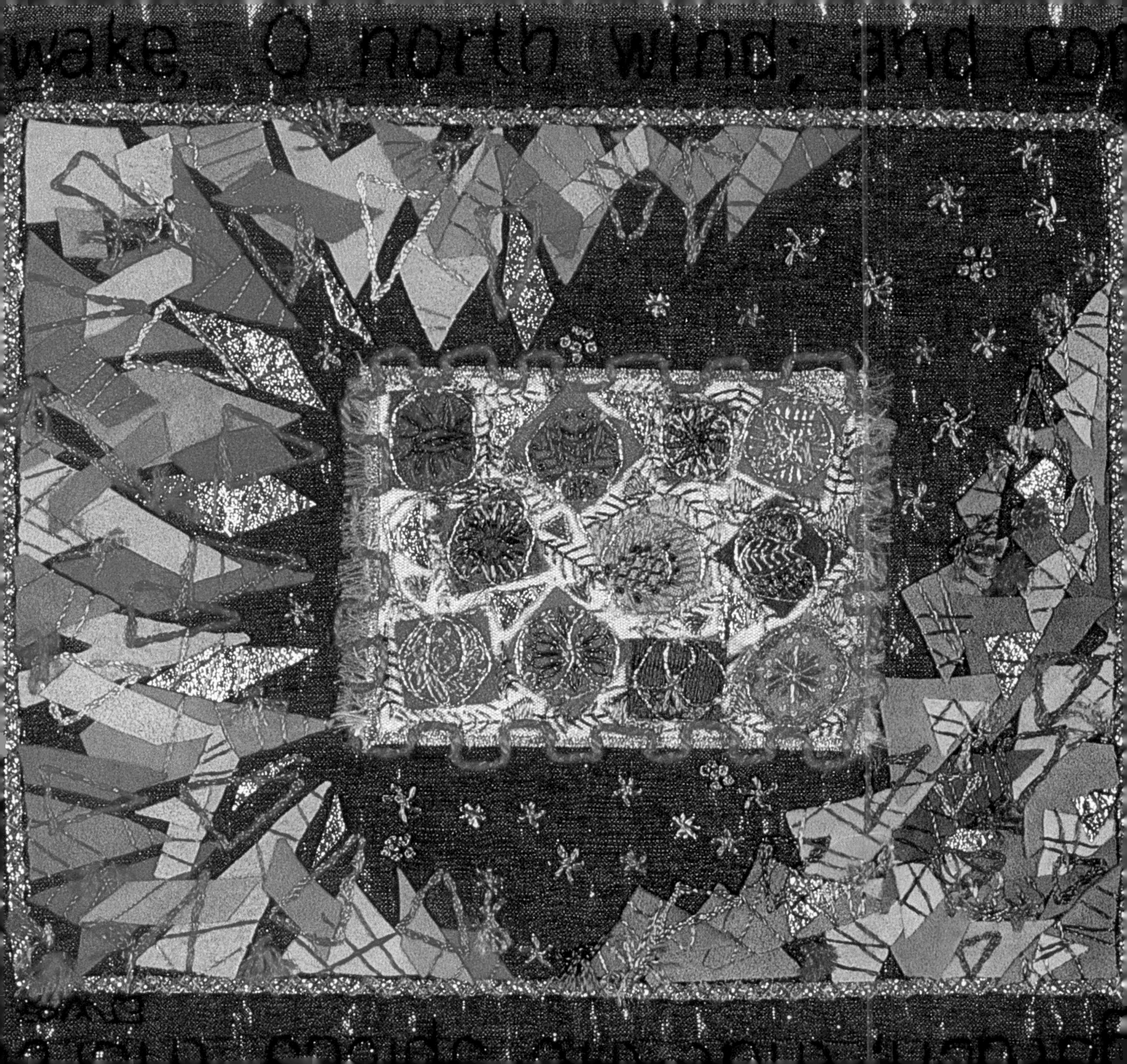
wake, O north wind; and co

MUSICAL BOX

CHAPTER 7

A method of approach

Every artist and crafts-person has his or her own methods of creating an image or achieving an object, from the 'roughing out' of a design in sketch form to the final moment of completion.

Perhaps you would like to follow the presentation outlined in this chapter for a creative stitchery project, and after the initial experience develop your own methods of approach.

Remember that you need never feel shy about using an illustration in whole or in part on which to base your early projects, especially if you are still finding your way with colour and design.

One method to choose a part of an illustration for a design.

A method for selecting a design

One way of selecting and securing an area within an illustration that appeals to you is to take a piece of black paper, perhaps 10 x 10 cm (4 x 4 in), and to cut a small hole in its centre. This could be circular or square, and about 3 cm (1¼ in) at its widest point. It is advisable to use black paper as it absorbs light and thus will not affect the colours that will be found along its perimeter, while white paper will reflect light and will slightly distort the colours that are closest to it. Do try this experiment. To find a suitable image for analysis move the opening within the black paper gradually around a colourfully printed page and pause on each occasion that you are attracted to the forms and the colours that fill the area.

The sketch

At this point you could make some rough sketches of each of the areas that attracts your attention, in a size that you feel comfortable to work with. Soon you will discover the kind of composition of shapes and colours that appeals to you most. By having applied colour in the form of wax or pencil crayons, fibre-tip pens, water-based paints, or even scraps of coloured paper torn out of magazine illustrations, you will have gained some idea of how to apply colour to a surface of paper. The transition from working on paper to working with threads and fabric in a stitched project will be almost effortless after this experience.

Whatever your subject matter may be, it is valuable to have a visual image in the form of a sketch, especially if it is in the dimensions that you wish your finished work to be. Your rough sketch will be a constant reminder of your first intentions. This will be very valuable if you are going to make the project a long-term one, or if your opportunities to stitch are infrequent.

Be creative!

At this point it is necessary to stress that there is no need to be a slave to the colours which you have selected. If those seen within the illustration do not correspond identically with the threads and fabric you have at hand, remember that it is at this point that creativity or invention take over from merely copying. Use what you have to gain a resemblance of what you see. Remember too that if you regard your early attempts at creative stitchery as an exercise, you will not suffer the anguish that is associated with trying to create a 'piece of art' right at the start of your endeavours. Because time is so precious, some feel that whatever stitchery project they are about to start must have a purpose, such as decorating a utilitarian object. One objection to this is that it prevents spontaneous experimentation, and thus removes the emphasis placed on the creative element within creative stitchery.

With the aid of your sketch and whatever illustrations you have chosen as a guide, collect the threads, or threads and fabrics that you feel are suitable for your project. This is also the time to gather the cords, braids, beads, sequins, net, gauze, transparent fabrics and metal threads which you may wish to incorporate into your stitched work.

First make a rough sketch (above left) of your design before you do colour exercises with pencil crayons (below left), water-colour (above right) or even a paper collage (below right).

A very useful tip is to make samples of certain areas of your design before you start working on the final piece. Any possible problems can be eliminated then and thus you will ensure the success of the end product.

Backing fabric

One valuable requirement is a backing fabric, preferably of well-washed, thin calico (muslin) or old, worn sheeting. This material should respond well to hand and machine stitching. The size of this piece should be larger than the area that you wish to work within, especially if you are going to use a stretching frame, whether it be circular or the square padded variety (see below). The value of the backing fabric is that it helps to give the foundation to your fabric collage design more body and prevents distortion when a lot of stitching is done in concentrated areas. A backing fabric is also valuable if you are going to do your work on a single-layered foundation fabric.

Frames that can be used for stitchery projects.

Frames

The decision whether or not to use a frame for your creative stitchery projects is a matter of personal preference. Remember though that it does help to keep the fabric taut and prevents it from puckering. If you wish, buy a hoop or tambour frame which consists of two circular frames, one fitting inside the other, the outer fitted with a screw to permit tightening. Once the fabric is stretched across the two frames the screw is tightened to hold the fabric taut.

Otherwise you can buy a square or rectangular frame or make it at home, either from a discarded picture frame, or from four pieces of wood secured at the corners with simple screw-on flat angle brackets. The foundation fabric can either be stapled to this structure, or you can pin your work tautly to the frame after covering it well with a layer of quilter's wadding or batting, and then with a generous 'bandage' of any suitable material (such as calico or muslin) which is then stitched together for security. There are advantages and disadvantages with this frame. Although the work can be removed easily and replaced quickly, it will not be as taut as when stapled to a frame.

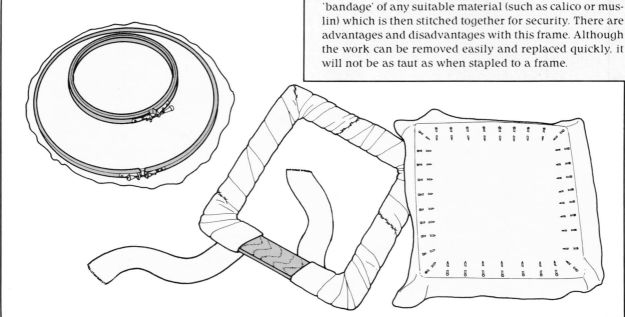

Samples

If you have time and are well-motivated, make a few samples of certain sections of the design, perhaps no bigger than 8 cm (3 in) square, before starting work on the final stitched piece. By using fabrics and stitches you feel are suitable for the design on a small format, you will be aware of the problems which you will encounter over a large area. One instructor under whom I studied, stressed the value of making several such samples before commencing the final full-scale piece. It was a valuable exercise, because we could change the colours and the design, and the amount of hand or machine stitchery planned for each area, at this point. In this way the success of the final piece was assured. Many might regard this as tedious, but it really is a highly instructive experience.

Enlarging a design

There are three methods of enlarging a design. The easiest is a free translation of your smaller sketch, but perhaps for some this may require some skill in drawing. The second method is widely available nowadays, namely to use a photocopying machine with which you can expand the image you have chosen to the size that you wish your end product to be.

Should this method not be available, then the method illustrated on the right is a little time-consuming, but the results will be more or less accurate. Over your image draw a grid with a ruler and an HB pencil, using letters and numbers in order to identify the lines. Then draw a diagonal line through the design. Place the design on the bottom left hand corner of a large sheet of paper and extend the diagonal line to the height you require. Complete the rectangle or square, divide it into the same amount of blocks as that on the original and add the letters and numbers. It is best to maintain accurate right angles throughout this process to prevent distortion. Transfer your design into this larger grid by plotting the points of the intersections of the design on the vertical and horizontal lines.

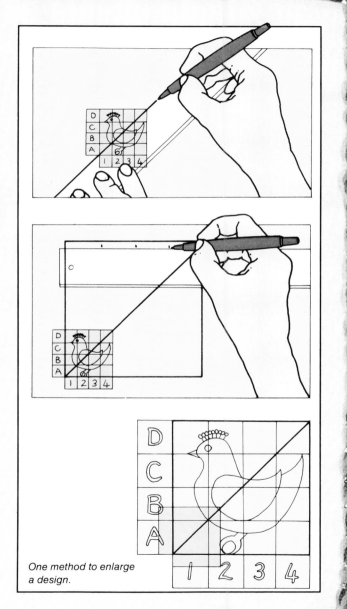

One method to enlarge a design.

A good method to transfer intricate designs from the sketch to the fabric.

Transferring the design from sketch to fabric

There are several methods for achieving this objective: the first I favour most and use myself; the second is recommended by many authorities; while others might prefer the third method which entails drawing straight on to the foundation fabric with a 'disappearing ink' or air-soluble pen. This leaves no residue, but it is advisable to work quickly as the image fades eventually.

For the first method, take a sheet of tracing paper and trace the main elements of the design on to it. Then square the design with the warp and weft threads of the foundation fabric. With the backing fabric beneath it, pin the tracing paper on to the two layers of the fabric. Use a sewing cotton or thread lighter in colour to the fabric you are going to work on, then tack (baste) with small running stitches around each form within your design. If you use a dark thread there is a danger that it will leave dark fibres behind when you pull it out which may be difficult to remove. When you have completed the tacking (basting stitches), run the point of a needle or pin carefully around the lines of stitching to make it easier to remove. Gently pull the tracing paper away from the fabric, and you will have a permanent design on your foundation material.

The alternative method is ideal for transferring intricate designs on to fabric. For this you will need tracing paper, on to which you have traced the design. Turn the tracing paper over and with a needle prick out the design, with the holes about 0.5 cm (¼ in) apart. Put a thick folded cloth beneath the tracing paper to ensure that you penetrate it. Then turn the tracing paper right side up and pin it on to the foundation fabric. Shake chalk over the design, ensuring that it penetrates the holes; a pad of fabric could facilitate this. Remove the tracing paper and join the dots with small stitches or with a fine paint brush and paint.

Templates for a fabric collage

A fabric collage is made up of pieces of coloured and textured fabrics cut to required shapes and placed into a design. To get the shapes you require, trace the design on to a piece of tracing paper and cut out the individual shapes. Place and pin each piece on the fabric of your choice and cut it out, allowing an extra margin of 3 to 4 mm (⅛ in) to ensure that all the components overlap and no unwanted background fabric is exposed. When you have assembled all the pieces, tack (baste) them down. At this point decide whether each piece will be hand or machine stitched on to the foundation fabric.

For those with skill it might not be necessary to cut paper templates; perhaps they have a flair for accurately cutting out pieces of fabric without going through the above procedure. The latter method could also be used by anyone if the design of the collage is quite simple.

Templates to cut out shapes in a design.

Stitches

This is the most exciting part of the design process, and can be done either by hand or on the sewing machine, or by using both methods in combination. Initially build up the overall design with stitches that form lines, or blocks of stitches which emphasize forms. Once this background has been established start working on broader details, such as thick and thin lines – produced with thick threads or many regular lines of stitching. Areas to be filled in could have one or two stitches repeated regularly, or one stitch repeated haphazardly.

Textures and delicate details should ideally be added at the end. Always remember that the concept of 'a stitch in time saves nine' is totally reversed in creative stitchery. For each stitch applied, there could in this art form be at least nine good reasons why more stitches should be added. From what I have experienced, an underdecorated piece of stitchery is far more common than an over-stitched piece.

Finishing off

Generally, all creative stitchers are happy with the outcome of their work, are keen to share their pleasure with others, and want to have their work framed.

Should slight distortion have taken place while you have been working on the fabric, it may be necessary to stretch it into shape before taking it to the framer or framing it yourself.

There are several methods of stretching your work to ensure a good finish. By following them you can eliminate the creases and wrinkles that may have appeared while you were working.

Pressing with a steam iron may sometimes be an appropriate method of finishing; however, this is not always advisable since it can flatten any 'feathery' textures, and it is highly unsuitable where beads have been used. In such a case, it will be necessary to block the design by gently pulling it into shape and securing it with drawing pins (thumb tacks). For this method you will need a piece of wood such as plywood or a piece of cardboard thick enough to withstand one or two sheets of damp blotting paper placed upon it. On the damp surface, place your work face upwards, and starting at the centre of one of the sides insert drawing pins (thumb tacks), making sure that the fabric grain is straight. Pull the opposite side of the work taut, and then insert drawing pins at even intervals. Treat the adjacent edges in the same manner, making sure that all of the wrinkles are removed.

Allow the work to dry out in a warm place before removing the pins.

Mounting a project

Requirements
- ☐ A piece of strong cardboard cut to the exact dimensions of your finished work.
- ☐ Stitched work with the backing fabric trimmed to within 5 cm (2 in) of the design.
- ☐ Strong thread, needle, scissors.

Method
Place the stitched piece face down on a flat surface and position the cardboard over it. Fold over the margins. With long lengths of sewing thread, preferably double, start in the centre of one of the sides, first completing the one half and then the other. Working towards the outside, lace the top and bottom margins together, thereby ensuring that the work is taut. Lace the right and left margins in the same manner. The work is now ready to be framed.

Hanging a project

This treatment is suitable for making up a design which should be hung to appreciate it fully.

Requirements
- ☐ Lining fabric.
- ☐ Non-woven interlining such as interfacing.
- ☐ Sewing thread, needles, scissors.
- ☐ Wooden dowel or metal tube for hanging the work.
- ☐ Webbing, of width appropriate to the diameter of the dowel or tube.

Method
Place the finished work face down on a flat surface with the trimmed interlining in place. Bring all the raw edges over the interlining and pin down. If there are any curved corners, snip the margin of the fabric and ease over the interlining. Carefully stitch all the turnings down with herringbone stitch, making sure that the stitches are not visible on the front of your work. Cut the lining to the required

Back of work showing how to mount it.

shape, allowing a 1,5-cm (¾ in) margin. Turn the margin in and secure with pins or tacking (basting) stitches. Place over the work and stitch into position. Stitch a length of webbing to the upper and lower edges of the work. Through the upper webbing place a dowel or tube for hanging purposes. A wooden lath threaded through the lower webbing will assist in an even mass distribution at the base of the work.

In this chapter various methods have been described to help you put creative stitchery into practice. Remember though that these are given as guidelines and that nothing stops you from developing your own methods.

The end result with the backing fabric behind it.

The Butterfl

The bright butterfli
species, exceeded onl
tera", the order's scien
winged", and tiny, shingl
and bodies of most adult
and moths vary more than
An owlet moth of South Am
the Eriocranid moth (below,
inch wingspan. Some species ar
There are no hard and fast
butterfly from a moth. But in gen
cocoons, butterflies do not. When a
tends to fold its wings like a tent wh
fly presses them together overhead. U
ly coloured and fatter bodied, the m
as a fluttering shadow in the d
unts its brilliance through

First they flew out and
colonized the adjacent
wall; later some migrated
to the screen.

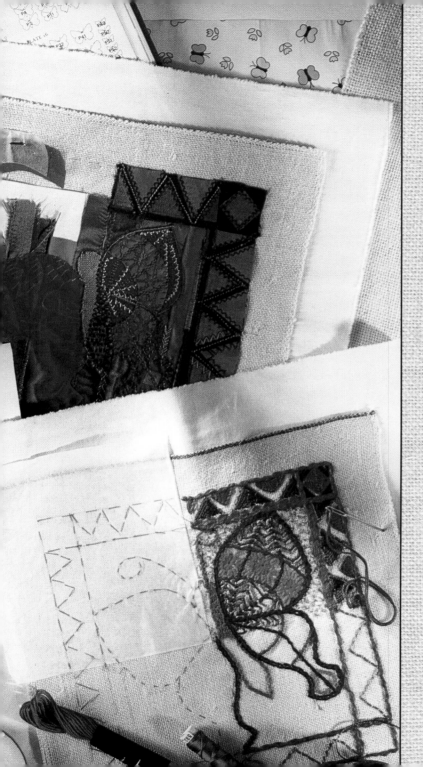

CHAPTER 8

Executing a design

Perhaps the easiest way to set off on a new venture is to use existing designs as a basis for your first projects. The fabric, colours and threads you use, as well as adding a personal touch here and there, will in any case lend originality and uniqueness to the work.
When you have gained enough confidence, you can give free rein to your imagination. By exploring every possibility you will not only be rewarded by an exciting piece of creative stitchery, but will also experience a very real sense of fulfilment.

The inspiration for the design used in this chapter came from several sources; geometric shapes, decorated tiles, and the butterfly from looking at a page of stamps on moths and butterflies. To achieve the shape of the butterfly within the square border, several cut-outs were made to ascertain the balance between background and butterfly. A sketch was then made which was used as a rough reference throughout for shapes and colour.

To start off with a stitching project, make some rough sketches and templates (below) of the design before doing a water-colour illustration (right).

Stitched piece

Requirements
- ☐ Two pieces of fabric (one for backing, the second for the foundation fabric).
- ☐ Tracing paper, pencil.
- ☐ Scissors, needles, pins, sewing thread.
- ☐ Matt, glossy, thick and thin threads in colours appropriate for the design.

Method
The foundation fabric was placed on top of the backing fabric and secured. The tracing paper with the design traced on to it was placed on the foundation fabric. It was squared up as closely as possible with the warp and weft threads, and then pinned down.

With a fine needle and sewing thread, tacking (basting) stitches were made around each shape within the design (Illustration: left hand top square). The tracing paper was

Creative stitchery with butterfly design showing how the different stages were executed.

gently pulled away and the tacking (basting) stitches became a permanent record of the design (left hand lower square). At this point the design was referred to and a variety of stitches used to outline the shapes within the design. The stitches used here are chain stitch, back stitch, stem stitch and couching (lower right hand square).

In the remaining square, detailed stitchery has been added. Consideration has been given to the use of matt, shiny, thick and thin threads, contrast of colours, and the use of stitches. Some lines have been made bolder, as seen in the border. Some areas have been filled in entirely, such as the wings and the body of the butterfly, while the area beside the wings has been tonally altered with the use of tiny stitches. The stitches used for detailed stitchery are buttonhole stitch, detached chain stitch, stem stitch and fly stitch on the wings of the butterfly, while buttonhole stitch was used on its body. The area beside the wings was filled in with seeding stitch. Triangles of fly stitch and buttonhole stitch were used to complete the border. A margin of white was left to provide a contrast in colours.

Stitched fabric collage

Requirements
- ☐ Tracing paper with the design traced on it.
- ☐ Two pieces of fabric, the backing and the foundation fabric.
- ☐ Scraps of coloured and textured fabric appropriate for the design.
- ☐ Coloured matt, shiny, thick and thin threads (also appropriate for the design).
- ☐ Needles, pins, scissors.
- ☐ Sewing machine.

Method
The foundation fabric was placed on top of the backing fabric. The traced shapes were cut out, one for each shape in the design. These were placed on to the appropriately coloured fabric and cut out, leaving a small margin of 3 to 4 mm (¼ in) to ensure an overlap.

For the background, strips of green and turquoise fabrics were sewn on to a soft fabric, using a sewing machine. The fabric was cut to size, and placed within the planned area (Illustration: top left hand square). After this strips of navy fabric were sewn down to form the border and the sections of the butterfly tacked (basted) into place (lower left hand square).

Two approaches to creative stitchery on a collage are demonstrated on the right hand side of the illustration. The lower right hand area is embellished with detailed hand stitching, with one to four threads in the needle at a time. The stitches on the background are feather stitch and fly stitch. On the butterfly's body, French knots and fly stitch were used, while the wing was set off with fly stitch, detached chain stitch, couching and seeding stitch. Fly stitch was used in the borders with the olive green stitching done on the sewing machine.

The creative stitchery in the upper right hand square was done almost entirely using a sewing machine. A limited variety of mechanical stitches is more than adequate. Even the zigzag alone is sufficient for creative stitchery on the sewing machine. Detached chain stitches were added by hand on the butterfly's wing.

The sketch, stitched design and stitched fabric collage illustrate how I approach the execution of a design. Before adding the final details to your own designs, consider the balance and weight of each shape within the whole design. Some areas could be left almost untouched, while others could be worked in great detail. This kind of attention should be paid not just to the motif in the centre, but to all the component parts of the stitched design, as well as to the frame itself. Sometimes it is interesting to add a sharp or extra bright colour to the central motif; this will undoubtedly draw the viewer's eye to this point. The problem with this kind of addition is that it tends to be where the eye will stop, so to make sure that all who view your work will see it in its entirety, make certain that flecks of the same colour are seen elsewhere in appropriate areas. What you must strive for is to take the viewer on a stimulating journey around your work!

This work illustrates beautifully how the same theme can, with a bit of imagination and experimentation, be given a totally new look. Using the same butterfly design as that on page 67, it was turned into a textile collage decorated with creative stitchery. The different steps show how the design was executed.

A final word

The emphasis of this book has been made clear at the outset – forget the rules! Disregard all the limitations that may have been freely passed on by too conservative teachers, family, friends and relations! Savour all the enthusiasm and suggestions that you can gather from those around you, who share your delight in working with fabric and creative stitchery. There are many enthusiasts around; all you have to do is to find them! With the theme 'forget the rules' in mind, explore and experiment with ideas and materials, and attempt to translate both into unorthodox forms. New materials are constantly being produced and apart from just being functional, most hold very exciting possibilities for creative exploration.

Left: Almost anything can be used in creative stitchery, from colourful textured fabrics and threads to beads, paper and leather as Faith Loy Plaut so aptly illustrates with this work, Lesotho Titana.

Eight chapters have been devoted to ways and means for introducing the uninitiated to creative stitchery, as well as encouraging broader horizons among those who are actively involved. Threads, fabric, colour and design combined are the important features in this art form. Linked with a flair for experimentation, it can only lead to interesting results.

At this stage of your reading you would probably have discovered where your creative interests lie. There are basically two groups of stitchers. One group will enjoy working through a number of experiments and exercises to gain the greatest satisfaction from the creative potential of familiar and unusual materials, allied to unorthodox means of reaching a desired result. The second group will be hesitant to experiment, yet will produce exciting work with traditional techniques as features. Whichever group you fall into, you will no doubt face the question of whether the work is complete or not. From my point of view a richly worked piece of stitchery is visually more exciting than one that is not.

May I wish you much pleasure as you explore the world of creative stitchery and realise the dimensions of your own creative abilities.

Bibliography

Beaney, J. *Embroidery: New Approaches*. Pelham Books, London, 1985.

Beaney, J. *Stitches: New Approaches*. B. T. Batsford Ltd., London, 1985.

Good Housekeeping Embroidery. Ebury Press, London, 1981.

Itten, J. *The Art of Colour*. Otto Maier, Ravensburg, 1973.

McNeil, M. *Machine Embroidery, Lace and See-through Techniques*.
B. T. Batsford Ltd., London, 1985.

Morrell, A. *Using Simple Embroidery Stitches*. B. T. Batsford Ltd., London, 1985.

Needlework School. *A comprehensive guide to decorative embroidery by
The Embroiderer's Guild Practical Study Group*. Windward, London, 1984.

Springall, D. *Embroidery. An introduction to the basic skills and techniques of the
craft*. British Broadcasting Corporation, London, 1980.

Thompson, M. *Dictionary of Embroidery Stitches*.
Hodder & Stoughton, London, 1934.